SUBMARINES

© Aladdin Books Ltd 1989

*First published in the
United States in 1989 by*
Gloucester Press
387 Park Avenue South
New York, NY 10016

ISBN 0-531-17153-1

Library of Congress Catalog
Card Number: 88-83095

Design David West
Children's Book Design

Editorial Lionheart Books

Researcher Cecilia Weston-Baker

Illustrators Peter Harper
Galina Zolfaghari

Printed in Belgium

CONTENTS

Underwater	4
Sorts of submarines	6
Sinking and rising	9
Steering	10
Creating the power	12
Finding the way	14
Looking and listening	16
Submarine detection	19
Hunter-killer submarines	21
Strategic weapons	22
Tactical weapons	24
Special submarines	26
History of submarines	28
Glossary	30
Index	32

HOW · IT · WORKS

SUBMARINES

IAN GRAHAM

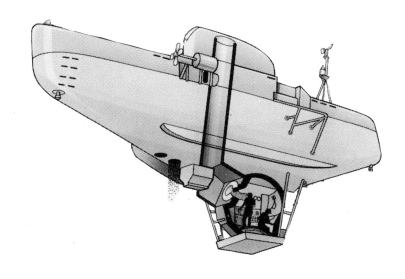

GLOUCESTER PRESS

New York · London · Toronto · Sydney

UNDERWATER

Submarines, or "subs", are boats that can travel underwater. They are built mainly for use by navies for attack and defense in war. But they are also used for deep sea exploration. In the future, they may be used as cargo vessels.

Submarines can dive hundreds of meters under the sea, where the crushing pressure of water is great. So for strength, the body, or hull, of subs has a double-layer design, with one hull inside the other. The outer hull is smooth and cigar-shaped to allow fast

SSN SWIFTSURE CLASS

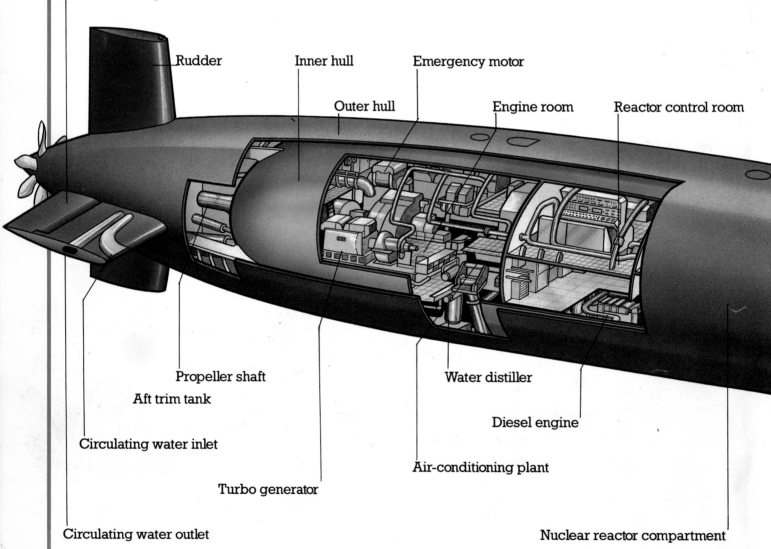

Rear stabilizing fin

Rudder

Inner hull

Emergency motor

Outer hull

Engine room

Reactor control room

Propeller shaft

Aft trim tank

Circulating water inlet

Turbo generator

Circulating water outlet

Water distiller

Diesel engine

Air-conditioning plant

Nuclear reactor compartment

movement through the water. This Swiftsure sub can travel at 30 knots (55km/h, 35mph) underwater.

A submarine must carry everything the crew needs until it can return to its base and take on fresh supplies. Air-conditioning equipment keeps the air clean. A water distiller turns salty seawater into fresh drinking water.

The power for this attack sub comes from a nuclear reactor. Heat produced by the reactor changes water into steam. The steam turns a pair of turbines, and the spinning turbines rotate the propeller that pushes the submarine through the water. The reactor must keep cool, and this is done by pumping seawater through it.

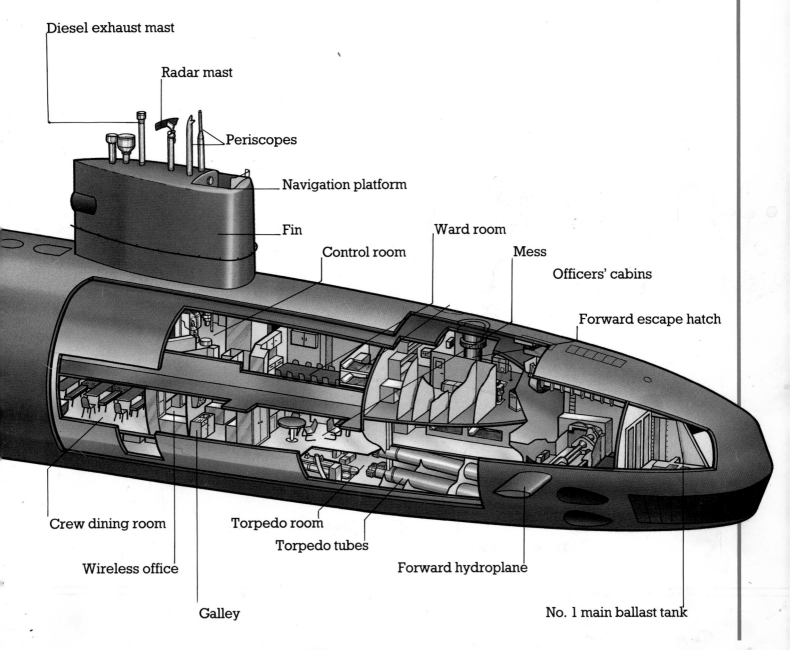

Diesel exhaust mast

Radar mast

Periscopes

Navigation platform

Fin

Ward room

Control room

Mess

Officers' cabins

Forward escape hatch

Crew dining room

Torpedo room

Torpedo tubes

Wireless office

Forward hydroplane

Galley

No. 1 main ballast tank

SORTS OF SUBMARINES

Most of the world's submarines are warships. They are designed to carry and fire torpedoes and missiles, or to lay mines, to destroy enemy vessels. Only the smallest submarines, called submersibles, are used for non-military, or civilian, work. Submersibles are built for repairing oil rigs, laying pipes on the seabed, and to study the underwater world.

There are two main types of submarine. The most common is the diesel-electric. This is powered by a diesel engine when on the surface of the water and by an electric motor when submerged. The second type is the nuclear submarine. This is powered at all times by a nuclear reactor. Diesel-electric submarines are the easiest and cheapest to build.

Military submarines are given code letters that describe their engines or the weapons they carry. For example, diesel-electric attack subs are coded SS, and nuclear powered ones SSN. Attack subs are designed to find and destroy enemy warships. Submarines that carry missiles which can be guided to a ship or target on land are coded SSG or, if nuclear powered, SSGN.

The nuclear powered hunter-killer submarine is fast and well-armed.

A submersible – for underwater research.

A nuclear missile-carrying submarine.

Submarines range in size from submersibles less than 6m (20ft) long to the 170m (558ft) Soviet Typhoon class submarine. This is nuclear powered and carries "ballistic" missiles (SSBN class).

A diesel-electric submarine.

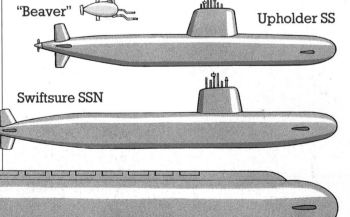

"Beaver"

Upholder SS

Swiftsure SSN

Typhoon SSBN

This submarine is blowing air out of its ballast tanks in order to dive.

Diving and surfacing

A submarine dives by taking in seawater to make it heavier. When the seawater is forced out again by compressed air, the submarine floats up to the surface.

Surfaced

Air

Seawater

Ballast tanks

Compressed air

Diving

Air out

Valves open

Seawater in   Valves open

Submerged

Valves closed

SINKING AND RISING

A submarine floats on the surface of the sea like a ship. To make it sink underwater, it must be made heavier than the water around it. This is done by opening valves to allow seawater to flood into tanks, called ballast tanks, located between the inner hull and the outer hull.

As the seawater rushes in through valves at the bottom of the ballast tanks, it pushes air out through valves at the top of the tanks. The seawater is heavier than the air it replaces and makes the submarine sink. By controlling the amount of water that flows into the ballast tanks, a submarine can be lowered to any depth and kept there.

Air can be pumped into the ballast tanks to force the water out again. The submarine, now lighter than the surrounding water, rises back to the surface. Water pressure on the submarine increases as it sinks. If a submarine continued to dive deeper and deeper, it would eventually be crushed by the water surrounding it.

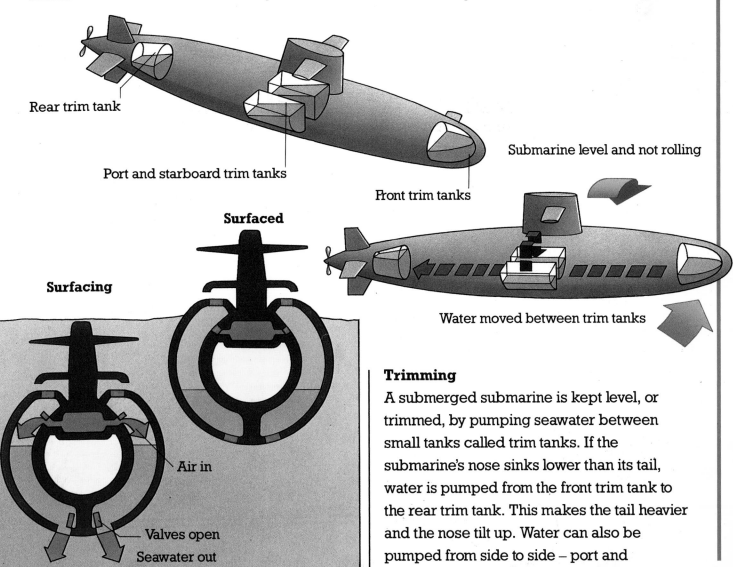

Submarine tilted down and front heavy

Rear trim tank

Port and starboard trim tanks

Front trim tanks

Submarine level and not rolling

Surfaced

Surfacing

Water moved between trim tanks

Air in

Valves open

Seawater out

Trimming

A submerged submarine is kept level, or trimmed, by pumping seawater between small tanks called trim tanks. If the submarine's nose sinks lower than its tail, water is pumped from the front trim tank to the rear trim tank. This makes the tail heavier and the nose tilt up. Water can also be pumped from side to side – port and starboard – to prevent rolling.

STEERING

A submarine is steered to the left and right by turning rudders on its tail, just as a surface ship is steered. But unlike a surface ship, a submarine also needs to maneuver up and down when it is underwater. Flooding and emptying its ballast tanks produces large changes in depth for diving and surfacing. But once a submarine has dived, hydroplanes are used to control its depth.

A hydroplane looks like a small aircraft wing. There are two pairs of hydroplanes – one pair at the front and the other at the back. When the hydroplanes are tilted up or down, the pressure of water against them as the submarine powers its way through the water forces the front or back of the vessel up or down. Because the action of hydroplanes depends on the force of water flowing across them, they only work when the submarine is moving.

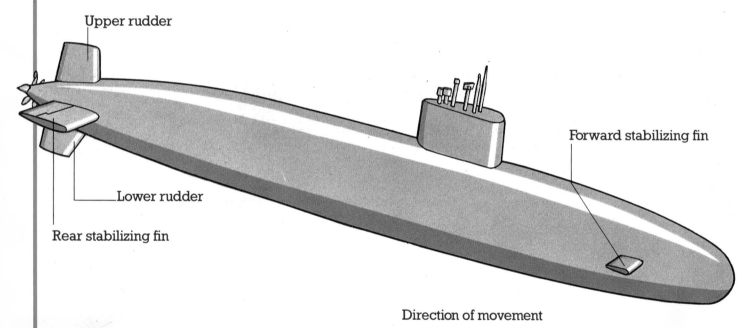

Upper rudder

Lower rudder

Rear stabilizing fin

Forward stabilizing fin

Steering underwater

If a submarine's front hydroplanes are tilted down and its back hydroplanes are tilted up, the whole submarine tilts nose-down. At this angle, its forward motion drives it deeper underwater.

If the front hydroplanes are tilted up and the back hydroplanes are tilted down, the nose comes up, the tail is forced down and the submarine rises again. The rudders are used to alter course to the left or right.

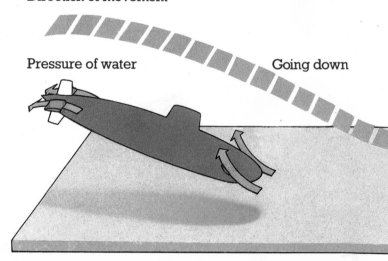

Direction of movement

Pressure of water

Going down

The submarine is steered by helmsmen who check the vessel's course on screens.

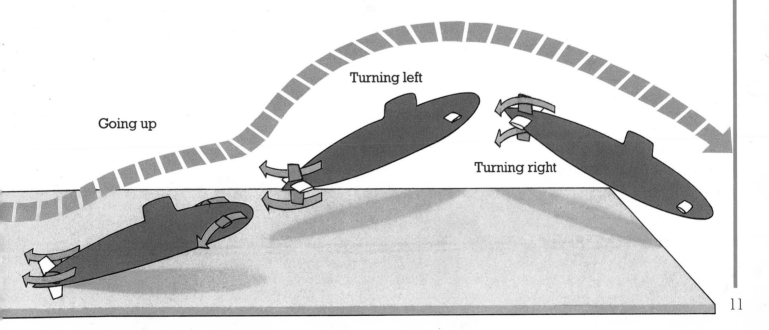

Going up

Turning left

Turning right

CREATING THE POWER

The smallest military submarines are fitted with diesel engines *and* electric motors. While these submarines are on the surface, the diesel engines provide propulsion (driving force) and charge the electric motors' batteries. Underwater, the "air-breathing" diesel engines are switched off and the battery-powered electric motor propels the submarine.

A diesel-electric sub must return to the surface to recharge its batteries. To avoid being attacked, it can do this without surfacing completely. The diesel engines suck in air through a "snorkel" tube.

Larger ocean-going submarines are nuclear powered. They do not have to surface regularly. The reactor provides all necessary power to propel the craft. The reactor may work for 500,000km (310,000 miles) before it needs to be refueled, compared to around 15,000km (9,000 miles) for diesel engines.

This nuclear sub has a 60,000 horsepower engine.

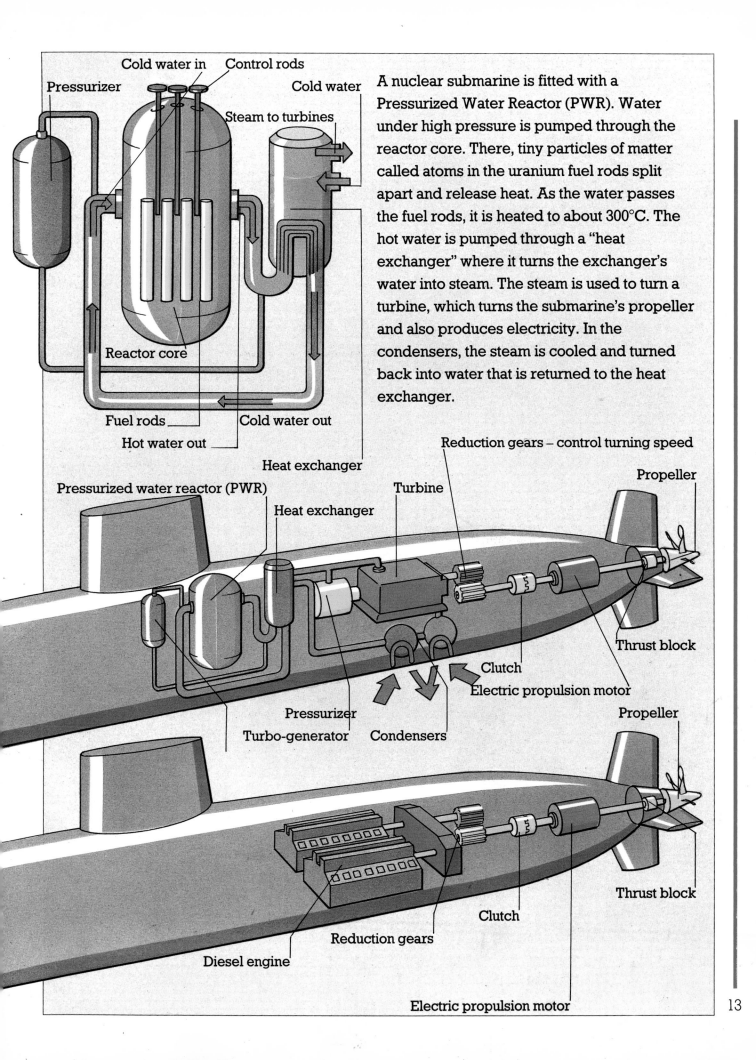

Cold water in   Control rods

Pressurizer

Cold water

Steam to turbines

A nuclear submarine is fitted with a Pressurized Water Reactor (PWR). Water under high pressure is pumped through the reactor core. There, tiny particles of matter called atoms in the uranium fuel rods split apart and release heat. As the water passes the fuel rods, it is heated to about 300°C. The hot water is pumped through a "heat exchanger" where it turns the exchanger's water into steam. The steam is used to turn a turbine, which turns the submarine's propeller and also produces electricity. In the condensers, the steam is cooled and turned back into water that is returned to the heat exchanger.

Reactor core

Fuel rods   Cold water out

Hot water out

Heat exchanger

Pressurized water reactor (PWR)

Heat exchanger

Reduction gears – control turning speed

Propeller

Turbine

Thrust block

Clutch

Electric propulsion motor

Pressurizer

Turbo-generator   Condensers

Propeller

Thrust block

Clutch

Reduction gears

Diesel engine

Electric propulsion motor

FINDING THE WAY

For a submarine to follow a course, or navigate, its position must always be known. Radar – short for radio detection and ranging – is normally used for this. The sub sends out radio signals. The signals bounce off objects in the water and these "echoes" are picked up by the vessel. A radar screen shows the outline of nearby coasts and ships, with the submarine at the center of the screen.

Within sight of land, the navigation officer can use the periscope to look for landmarks such as mountains or light-houses, and compare their bearings with their actual positions on a map. He can also navigate by the stars and Moon at night and by the Sun during the day. Their positions in the sky appear to vary depending on the submarine's location. By taking accurate sightings of them, the submarine's position can be calculated.

All these methods of navigation rely on the submarine surfacing or coming up to periscope depth. A system called the Ship's Inertial Navigation System (SINS) is entirely electronic. It shows the submarine's position without the need to surface or for any sightings of Sun, stars, Moon or landmarks.

It is important not only that subs stay on course, but also keep in contact with friendly ships and aircraft without making their positions known to the enemy. Most military communications use special "high-frequency" radio signals. But, from the direction of a submarine's radio signals, enemy ships can find the bearing of the sub. For this reason, special ways of transmitting and receiving very low-frequency radio messages have been developed for use by subs when underwater.

SINS calculates a moving submarine's position using gyroscopes and accelerometers. A gyroscope is like a spinning top. As it spins, it pushes against any movement of the sub that tries to tip it over. The force of the push can be measured. An accelerometer measures acceleration, that is, how quickly the sub changes speed. SINS uses three gyroscopes, one for each of three directions – north-south, east-west and up-down. When the sub turns or submerges, the gyroscopes move and accelerometers measure the amount of movement. A computer compares the instruments' measurements to calculate how far the sub has traveled in each of the three directions. SINS is fully automatic and works nonstop. It is also extremely accurate.

Ship's Internal Navigation System (SINS)

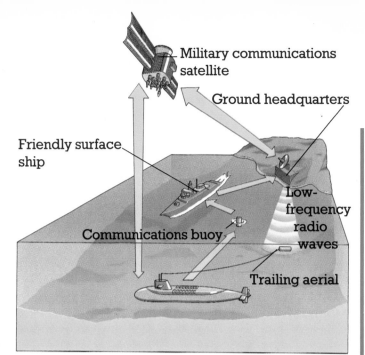

Military communications satellite

Ground headquarters

Friendly surface ship

Low-frequency radio waves

Communications buoy

Trailing aerial

A navigation officer watches an instrument panel showing the submarine's position.

A sub can communicate without surfacing by allowing only a radio aerial to break the surface, or by releasing a communications buoy. The floating buoy sends out signals to ships nearby. Subs can also send and receive signals via satellites. Special "low-frequency" radio signals can travel through water. Subs receive these signals by trailing an aerial cable through the water.

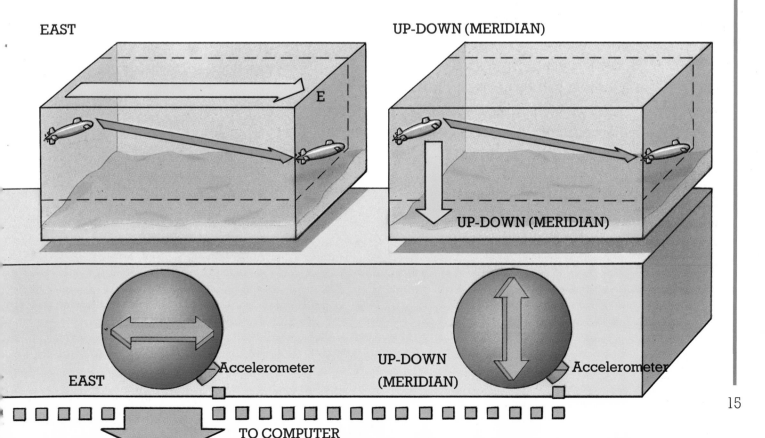

EAST

E

UP-DOWN (MERIDIAN)

UP-DOWN (MERIDIAN)

EAST

Accelerometer

UP-DOWN (MERIDIAN)

Accelerometer

TO COMPUTER

LOOKING AND LISTENING

Without specially developed looking and listening equipment, a submerged submarine would be unable to detect other vessels and obstacles in the sea around it. It could not be navigated safely through the seaways or detect an enemy nearby.

Near the surface, a periscope is used to give a view of the surrounding sea as far as the horizon. Radar is also used to scan the sea surface and the sky for ships and aircraft. Deeper underwater, below about 18m (59ft), neither the periscope nor radar can be used. Instead, a submarine uses sonar.

Like radar, sonar works by sending out signals and detecting their echoes. Radar uses radio signals, but sonar uses short bursts, or pulses, of sound. Underwater microphones, called hydrophones, attached to the sub's hull, pick up sound reflections from the seabed, ships, and other objects like icebergs.

Most of a submarine's sonar sensors are placed around the front of the hull to give early warning of obstacles in the sub's path.

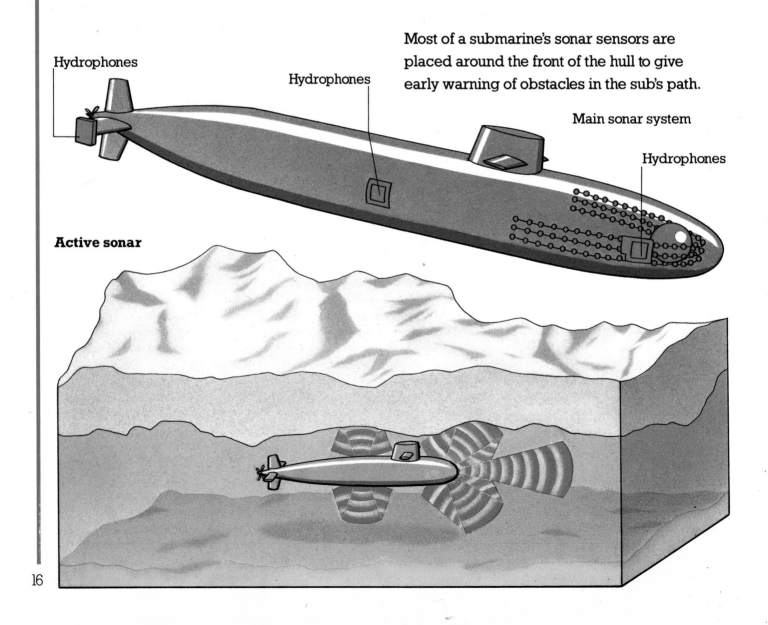

Hydrophones

Hydrophones

Main sonar system

Hydrophones

Active sonar

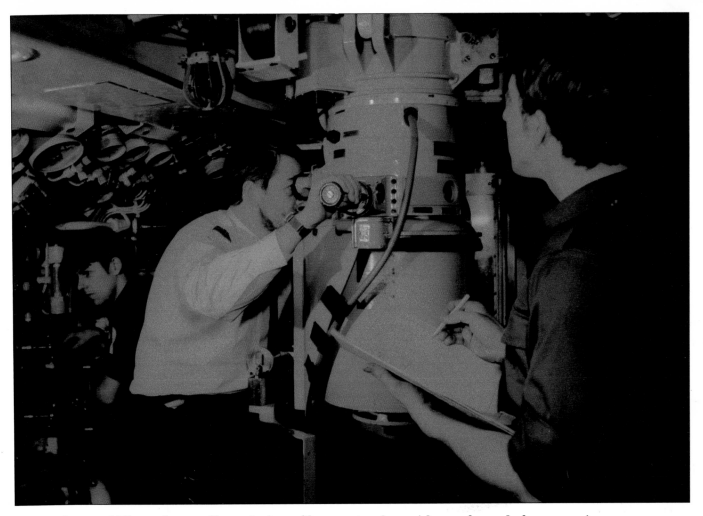

Up periscope! There is usually a choice of lenses to give wide angle and close-up views.

Sonar can be used in one of two ways. Pulses of sound sent out from "transducers" on the hull bounce off anything solid near the submarine. Hydrophones pick up the echoes. This is active sonar (below left).

Enemy submarines can detect active sonar. One answer is to switch off the sound transmitters and use the hydrophones to pick up engine and other sounds from enemy vessels. This is passive sonar (below).

Passive sonar

A U.S. Navy helicopter lowers a submarine-detecting sonar buoy toward the water below.

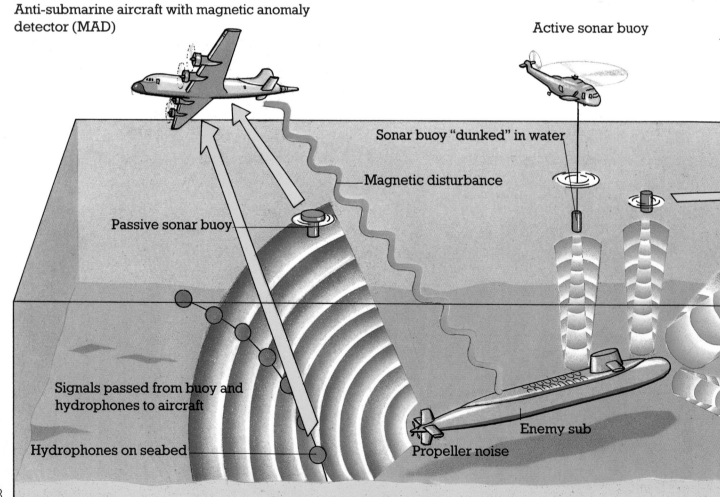

Anti-submarine aircraft with magnetic anomaly
detector (MAD)

Active sonar buoy

Sonar buoy "dunked" in water

Magnetic disturbance

Passive sonar buoy

Signals passed from buoy and
hydrophones to aircraft

Hydrophones on seabed

Propeller noise

Enemy sub

SUBMARINE DETECTION

Submarines are a serious threat in wartime. Not only can they attack and destroy other submarines and surface vessels, they can also inflict serious damage to military and civilian targets on land. It is important to be able to find enemy subs so that they can be dealt with swiftly and effectively.

All submarines make noises that can be picked up by sonar systems. For this reason, submarine designers are always trying to make the vessels work more quietly. Even if noises from inside the submarine – the whirring of motors and pumps – are cut down, propeller noise is difficult to eliminate. As the propeller spins around, it churns up the water and makes noise. As the sub travels through the water, any roughness on the hull, such as the edge of a hatch, stirs up the water and causes noises that a sonar system can detect. Sonar operators are trained to recognize the difference between echoes from shoals of fish and those from surface ships and submarines. Submarines also produce magnetic effects that can be detected by sensors in aircraft.

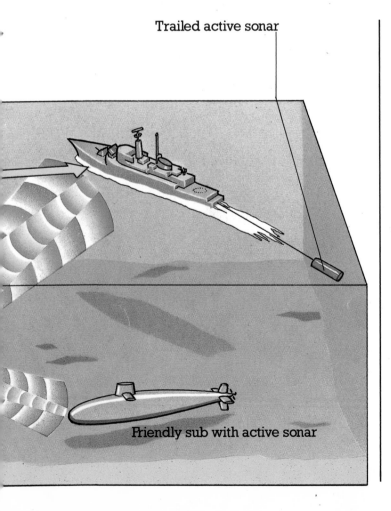

Trailed active sonar

Friendly sub with active sonar

An Anti-Submarine Warfare (ASW) group at work. Helicopters hover over the sea and dip sonar buoys into the water, a technique called dunking. Hydrophones planted on the seabed or dropped into the sea by helicopters listen for sounds from enemy submarines.

Friendly submarines use active sonar to detect hostile craft underwater. (During wartime, submarines do not use their radar navigation systems as the radar signals can be easily detected by enemy vessels and aircraft.) On the surface, a ship uses a sonar buoy, trailed through the water behind it (to reduce noise from the ship itself).

A submarine is such a large metal structure that it disturbs the Earth's magnetic field as it moves along. An aircraft circling overhead carries a Magnetic Anomaly Detector (MAD), which detects this effect to locate subs.

Together, an ASW group is likely to locate an enemy sub within a few minutes.

An Ikara radio-controlled aircraft with homing torpedo is being prepared for launch.

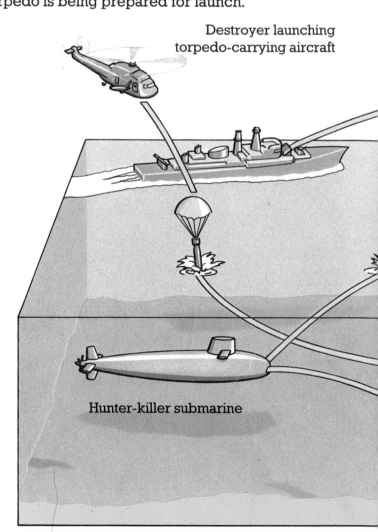

Destroyer launching torpedo-carrying aircraft

Hunter-killer submarine

An enemy submarine has been detected. Destroyer ships, helicopters and a hunter-killer sub move in to attack it.

The hunter-killer may fire a "homing" torpedo, which uses its own sonar to follow and hit the target submarine. It might also fire Subroc (short for submarine-launched rocket), a nuclear weapon with a range of 56km (35 miles). Subroc leaves the water and flies fast towards its target before diving into the sea and exploding at a set depth.

Destroyers on the surface drop depth charges, which also explode at a set depth. Or they launch radio-controlled aircraft that fly over the target and drop a homing torpedo into the water. Homing torpedoes can also be dropped from helicopters.

HUNTER-KILLER SUBMARINES

One type of submarine, called an attack sub or "hunter-killer," is used to seek out and destroy enemy submarines and surface ships. It can also be used to protect friendly ships from attack.

In wartime, large amounts of supplies for armies and civilians are transported by sea. One of the hunter-killer submarine's most important wartime jobs is to stop enemy supplies getting through while protecting friendly supply ships.

The world's first nuclear hunter-killer submarine (code SSN) was the USS *Tullibee*, built in 1960. Some of the *Tullibee*'s design features are still used today in the most modern nuclear powered hunter-killer subs, such as the United States' *Los Angeles*. Built in 1976, the *Los Angeles* weighs 6,000 tons and carries a crew of 127. When an enemy submarine or ship is detected, the hunter-killer sub can use a range of weapons against it.

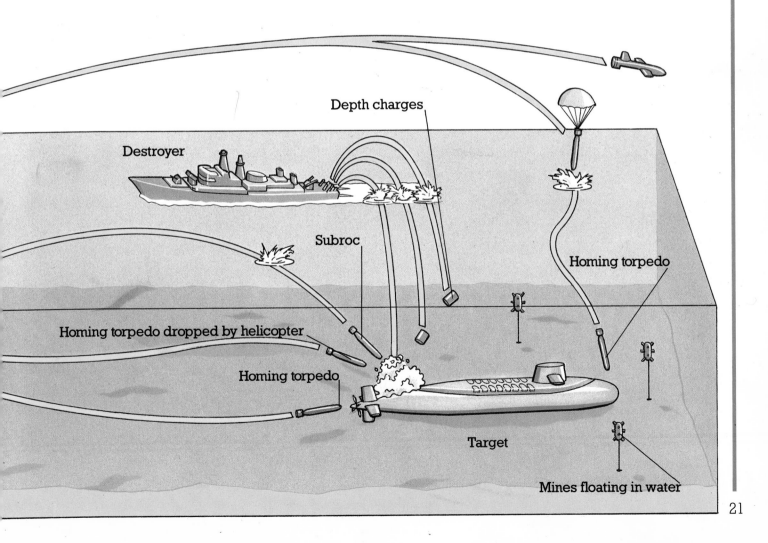

Depth charges

Destroyer

Subroc

Homing torpedo

Homing torpedo dropped by helicopter

Homing torpedo

Target

Mines floating in water

STRATEGIC WEAPONS

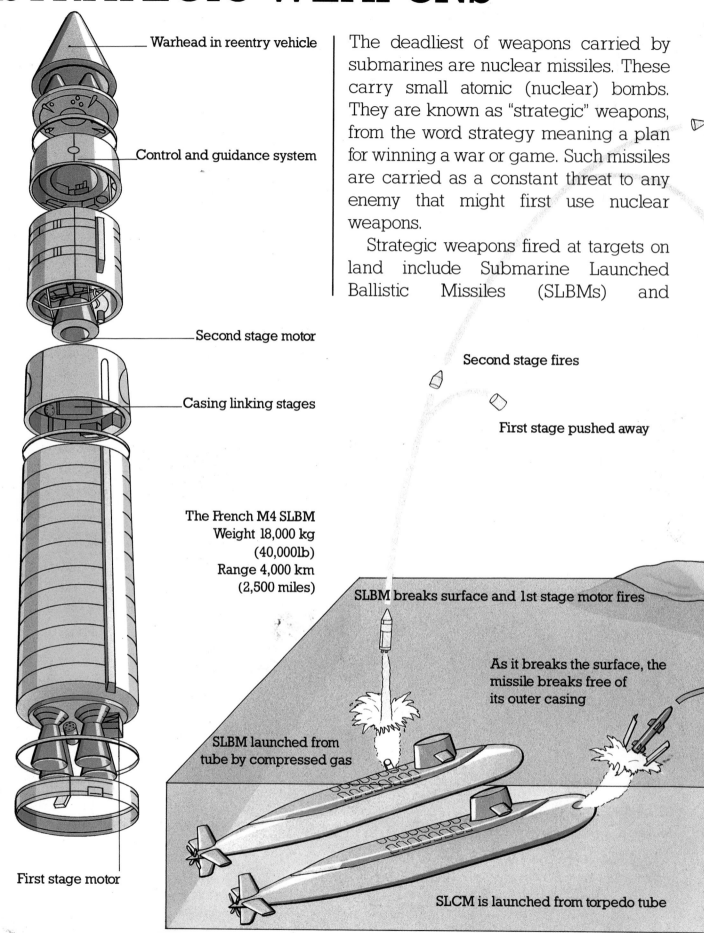

Warhead in reentry vehicle

Control and guidance system

Second stage motor

Casing linking stages

The French M4 SLBM
Weight 18,000 kg
(40,000lb)
Range 4,000 km
(2,500 miles)

First stage motor

The deadliest of weapons carried by submarines are nuclear missiles. These carry small atomic (nuclear) bombs. They are known as "strategic" weapons, from the word strategy meaning a plan for winning a war or game. Such missiles are carried as a constant threat to any enemy that might first use nuclear weapons.

Strategic weapons fired at targets on land include Submarine Launched Ballistic Missiles (SLBMs) and

Second stage fires

First stage pushed away

SLBM breaks surface and 1st stage motor fires

As it breaks the surface, the missile breaks free of its outer casing

SLBM launched from tube by compressed gas

SLCM is launched from torpedo tube

Submarine Launched Cruise Missiles (SLCMs). An SLBM has several stages. When the fuel in one stage is used up, the fuel tank and its rocket motors drop away and the next stage takes over. An SLBM flies high above the Earth's atmosphere. When it reenters the atmosphere, it releases many separate warheads, each aimed at a different target. SLCMs fly low, following the shape of the ground to avoid detection by enemy radar.

Missile unit releases warheads on to targets

Second stage pushed away

A Submarine Launched Cruise Missile (SLCM)

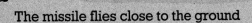

The missile flies close to the ground

SLBMs can strike targets 7,000km (4,300 miles) away. SLCMs have a range of about 2,500km (1,500 miles). "Ballistic" missiles fall under gravity (the Earth's pull) once their fuel is used up. "Cruise" missiles swerve like an aircraft.

TACTICAL WEAPONS

Weapons used by one vessel against another are called tactical weapons. They are smaller and have a shorter range than strategic weapons. They include torpedoes, antisubmarine missiles and anti-ship cruise missiles.

The torpedo shown below has a sonar system for finding and following its target. Alternately, information about the target's position can be sent from the submarine to its torpedo along a wire connecting the two. "Smart" torpedoes can detect when they have missed their target, then double back to try to hit it again. Simpler torpedoes similar to those used in World War II are still in use today. Once fired, they continue in a straight line at the same depth.

The fastest nuclear sub can travel faster than a torpedo, and so missiles such as Subroc must be used to destroy them. Submarines can also use missiles to attack ships. "Harpoon" is a cruise missile that flies just above the waves for up to 110km (68 miles).

US Mark 48 torpedo

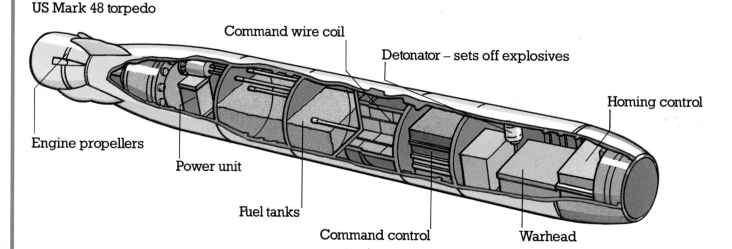

Command wire coil

Detonator – sets off explosives

Homing control

Engine propellers

Power unit

Fuel tanks

Command control

Warhead

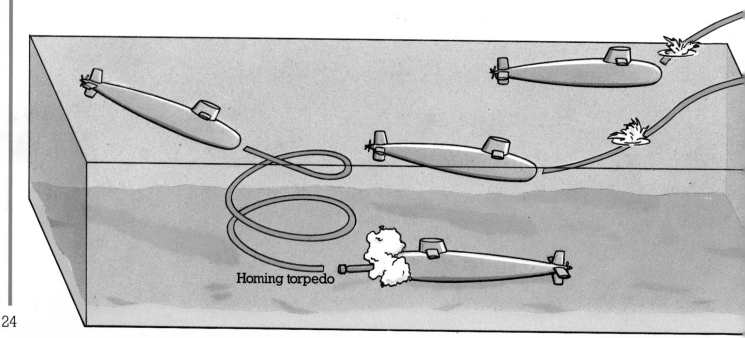

Homing torpedo

In the torpedo room, the crew get ready to fire the sub's underwater weapons.

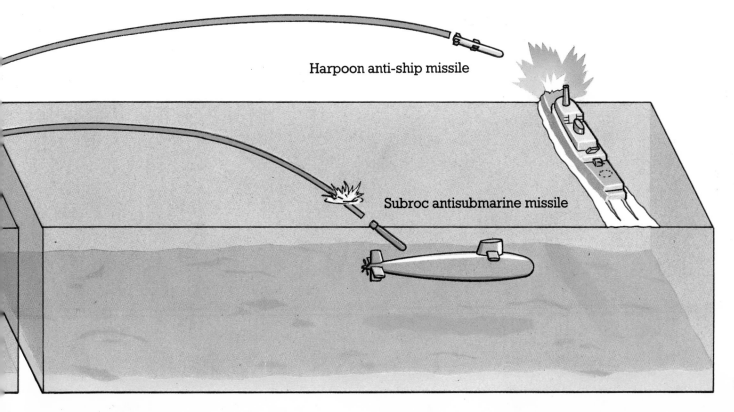

Harpoon anti-ship missile

Subroc antisubmarine missile

SPECIAL SUBMARINES

Some submarines are specially designed to do a particular job. Small submarines, or submersibles, are used to inspect underwater pipelines and telephone cables. They may be fitted with robot arms to enable the crew to pick things up and bring them back to the surface. Other craft, known as Deep Submergence Rescue Vehicles (DSRVs), are designed to connect to a submarine's escape hatch so that the crew of a damaged submarine can be rescued.

Submersibles also help scientists to investigate the deepest parts of the world's oceans. Deep underwater it is very dark and the water is at great pressure. Deep-diving craft must carry their own lights and must be strengthened to resist the crushing water pressure. The submersible *Alvin* was used to photograph the wreck of the passenger ship *Titanic*. The *Titanic* sank after hitting an iceberg on its first voyage across the Atlantic in 1912. *Alvin's* titanium (an especially strong metal) hull enabled it to dive to 4,000m (14,000ft) just enough to reach the floor of the Atlantic Ocean where the *Titanic* lay. A French craft, *Trieste*, has made the deepest dive 11,000m (38,500ft) to the bottom of the Pacific Ocean.

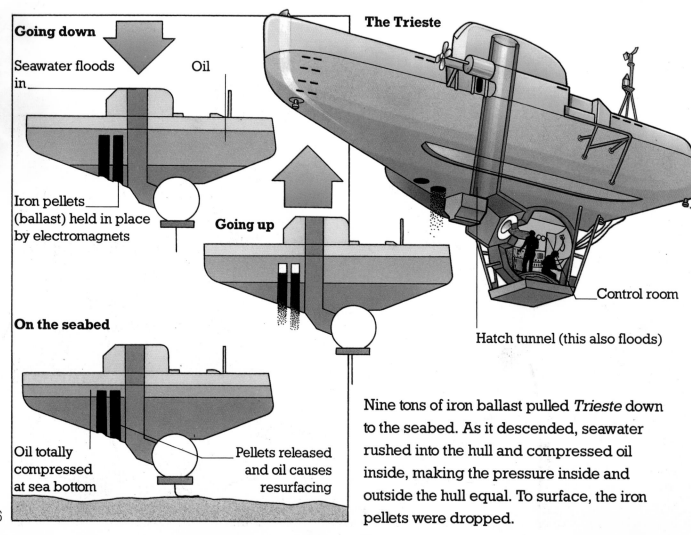

Going down

Seawater floods in

Oil

Iron pellets (ballast) held in place by electromagnets

Going up

On the seabed

Oil totally compressed at sea bottom

Pellets released and oil causes resurfacing

The Trieste

Control room

Hatch tunnel (this also floods)

Nine tons of iron ballast pulled *Trieste* down to the seabed. As it descended, seawater rushed into the hull and compressed oil inside, making the pressure inside and outside the hull equal. To surface, the iron pellets were dropped.

A deep sea submersible explores the seabed using lights and cameras.

Inside the control unit of a submersible.

HISTORY OF SUBMARINES

Early days

The first military submarine was designed in the 1770s by an American David Bushnell. It was built to attack British ships during the Revolutionary War. It was to be steered beneath a ship and an explosive charge attached to the ship's hull. The attempt failed, however.

The Turtle – the first sub used in war.

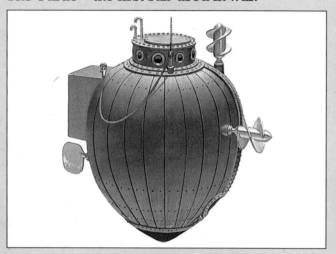

In the 1800s, there were two important advances in submarine technology. The *Nautilus*, designed by another American, Robert Fulton, in 1800, was the first submarine to have a metal hull. Then in the 1890s the Irish-American, John P. Holland, built a submarine powered by an internal combustion engine (an automobile engine) when on the surface and by an electric motor when submerged. This efficient combination produced the first successful long-distance submarine.

1900-1950

Submarines were first used in large numbers during World War I (1914-1918). There were about 400 submarines in service with the world's navies. By then, the gasoline-fueled engines used by earlier submarines had

A U-boat and crew return to port.

been replaced by engines using safer diesel oil. Submarines such as the successful German Unterseeboote, or U-boats, could attack ships with torpedoes.

During World War II (1939-1945) submarines were again very successful in sinking supply ships. Electronic aids such as active sonar, developed during the war, made it easier to detect enemy submarines. Work on nuclear weapons during the war led to the development

Nautilus – the first nuclear submarine.

of nuclear reactors instead of diesel engines for generating power.

1950-present-day

In 1954, the first submarine to use a nuclear power plant, the USS *Nautilus*, was launched. Unlike diesel-electric submarines, which have to return to the surface regularly to charge their batteries, nuclear submarines can remain submerged for thousands of miles.

The only nuclear submarine that has ever carried out an attack is Britain's HMS *Conqueror*, which in 1982 sank the Argentinian battleship *General Belgrano* during the Falklands War.

A Soviet Typhoon class SSBN

In the future, designers will attempt to make submarines even quieter than they are now in order to avoid detection. The greatest advances are likely to be made in electronic warfare, with new ways of escaping the submarine hunters. From the 1990s onward, new classes of submarines will be able to dive deeper and faster.

GLOSSARY

air supply
To obtain fresh air underwater a submarine is fitted with a special electrical device known as an electrolysis machine (see diagram, right). Electrolysis is a process for splitting certain chemicals into their component parts, such as water into oxygen and hydrogen gases. An electric current is passed through the water. Oxygen bubbles up at the positive terminal, where it is collected and added to the air as required.

ballast tanks
Tanks inside a submarine that are filled with seawater to submerge the craft and emptied again to make it float up to the surface.

ballistic
A missile that follows a high, curving flight path then plunges down on to its target.

class
A series of submarines built to the same design.

cruise missile
A winged missile that is usually powered by a jet engine and fitted with an electronic guidance system. Cruise missiles fly low over water and land to avoid detection by radar.

dead reckoning
A method of navigation in which a vessel's current position is calculated from its last known position, speed, course and tides.

depth charge
An antisubmarine bomb dropped from a ship or aircraft. It explodes when it reaches a certain depth in the water.

high-frequency radio waves
The frequency of a wave measures how many complete waves there are each second. This can be many thousands in the case of high-frequency (HF) radio.

hydrophone
A microphone used to pick up sounds underwater.

hydroplane
A wing-like fin that can be tilted up or down to alter a submarine's depth.

periscope
An instrument that uses mirrors, lenses and prisms to give its operator in a submerged submarine a view of the sea and sky (see diagram).

propeller
A submarine's means of propulsion. The angled blades of the rotating propeller convert engine power into a force that pushes the sub through the water.

radar
RAdio Detection And Ranging. Radio waves are transmitted in all directions. The direction of any waves that bounce back (echoes) and the time they take to

return reveal the position of the object that they strike.

sonar
SOund NAvigation Ranging. The use of sound waves to detect objects near a submarine.

SS
A diesel-electric submarine.

SSBN
A nuclear powered submarine carrying ballistic missiles.

SSG
A diesel-electric submarine equipped with cruise (guided) missiles.

SSGN
A nuclear powered cruise missile submarine.

SSN
A nuclear powered hunter-killer submarine.

torpedo
A motorized underwater missile. Homing torpedoes track and strike moving targets whichever way they move.

trim tanks
Tanks inside a submarine used to keep the submarine level underwater by pumping water from one tank to another.

warhead
The explosive part of a missile.

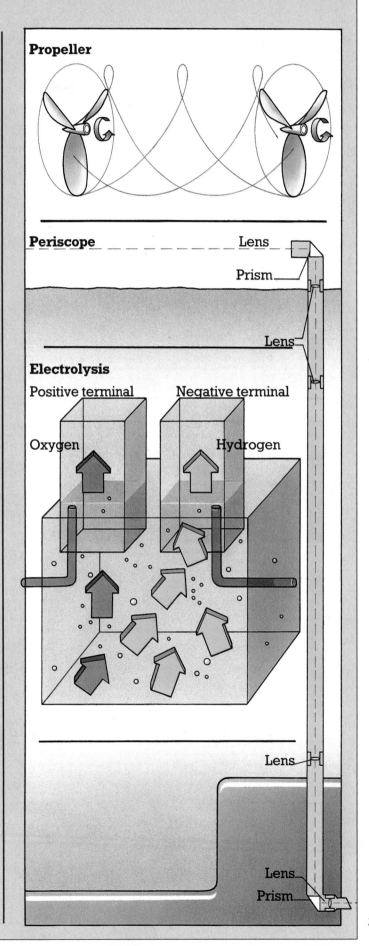

INDEX

accelerometers 14, 15
active sonar 17, 19, 28
aerials 5, 15
air-conditioning 4, 5, 30
Alpha Class subs 29
Alvin 26
ASW 19
attack subs 4, 5, 6

ballast 26
ballast tanks 8, 9, 10, 30
ballistic missiles 7
batteries 12
"Beaver" sub 7
Bushnell, David 28

cargo vessels 4
clutch 13
communications 15
condensers 13
control room 4
cooling system 5
crew 5

defense subs 4
depth of travel 9, 10, 16, 26, 29
depth charges 20, 21, 30
diesel-electric subs 6, 7, 12
diesel exhaust mast 5
diving 8, 9, 10
DSRVs 26
dunking sonar 18, 19

echoes, radar 14, 17, 19
engine room 4
exploration subs 4

fins 5
forward escape hatch 5
fuel 12, 13
Fulton, Robert 28

gyroscopes 14

"Harpoon" 24
heat exchanger 13
high-frequency signals 14
HMS Conqueror 29
Holland, John P. 28
homing torpedoes 21
hull 4, 9, 16, 19
hunter-killer subs 6, 20, 21
hydrophones 16, 17, 18, 19, 30
hydroplanes 10, 30

Ikara aircraft 20

Los Angeles Class subs 21, 29
low-frequency signals 15

MAD system 18, 19
motors 4, 6, 12
missiles 7, 22, 23, 24

navigating 14, 15
navigation platform 5
nuclear reactor 4, 5
nuclear subs 6, 12, 29

passive sonar 17
periscope 5, 14, 16, 17, 30
propeller 5, 13, 19, 30
propeller shaft 4
propulsion 12, 13
PWR power source 13

radar 5, 14, 16, 30
radar mast 5
reduction gears 13
reactor compartment 4
reactor core 13
rear stabilizing fin 4
repair subs 6

rolling in water 9
rudders 4, 10, 16

SINS 14
size 7, 12, 29
SLBMs 22, 23
SLCMs 22, 23
sonar 16, 19, 28, 30
speed 5, 29
SSs 6, 30
SSBNs 6, 30
SSGs 6, 30
SSNs 6, 20, 30
stabilizing fins 4, 10
steam 5, 13
steering 10, 11
submersibles 6, 7, 26
Subroc 20, 21, 24
surfacing 8, 9, 10
Swiftwure sub 5, 7

tactical weapons 24
thrust block 13
torpedoes 6, 20, 21, 24, 30
torpedo room 5, 25
torpedo tubes 5, 22
transducers 17
Trieste subs 26, 29
trimming 9
trim tanks 9, 30
turbines 9, 13
turbo generator 4, 13
Turtle sub 28, 29
Typhoon Class subs 7, 29

U-boats 28
underwater research subs 7
Upholder sub 7
USS Tullibee 21

weapons 21, 22, 23, 24, 28

Photographic credits

Cover and pages 6, 7 (top left), 8, 12, 15, 18 and 28 (bottom): Salamander Books; pages 7 (bottom right) and 27 (both): Planet Earth Pictures; pages 7 (bottom), 11 and 17: MoD RN PR; page 23: MARS/General Dynamics; page 25: MARS/MoD RN; page 28 (top): Popperfoto